The Legend of the Pied Piper

Gareth Stevens
PUBLISHING

By
Katherine Ponka

Please visit our website, www.garethstevens.com. For a free color catalog of all our high-quality books, call toll free 1-800-542-2595 or fax 1-877-542-2596.

Library of Congress Cataloging-in-Publication Data

Ponka, Katherine.
 The Legend of the Pied Piper / Katherine Ponka.
    pages cm. — (Famous Legends)
 Includes bibliographical references and index.
 ISBN 978-1-4824-2740-0 (pbk.)
 ISBN 978-1-4824-2741-7 (6 pack)
 ISBN 978-1-4824-2742-4 (library binding)
 1. Pied Piper of Hamelin (Legendary character) I. Title.
 PN57.P5P66 2015
 809'.93351—dc23
                                                    2014048094

First Edition

Published in 2016 by
Gareth Stevens Publishing
111 East 14th Street, Suite 349
New York, NY 10003

Copyright © 2016 Gareth Stevens Publishing

Designer: Laura Bowen
Editor: Therese Shea

Photo credits: Cover, p. 1 (pied piper illustration) Robert Browning/Bridgeman Art Library/Getty Images; cover, p. 1 (ribbon) barbaliss/Shutterstock.com; cover, p. 1 (leather) Pink Pueblo/Shutterstock.com; cover, pp. 1–32 (sign) Sarawut Padungkwan/Shutterstock.com; cover, pp. 1–32 (vines) vitasunny/Shutterstock.com; cover, pp. 1–32 (parchment) TyBy/Shutterstock.com; cover, pp. 1–32 (background) HorenkO/Shutterstock.com; p. 5 Alexander Ishchenko/Shutterstock.com; p. 7 DEA Picture Library/De Agostini/Getty Images; p. 9 (main) Westend61/Getty Images; p. 9 (inset) Map Lab/Wikimedia Commons; p. 11 loki11/Wikimedia Commons; p. 13 (main) Kate Greenaway/Wikimedia Commons; p. 13 (inset) Yangchao/Shutterstock.com; pp. 15, 21 Print Collector/Hulton Archive/Getty Images; p. 17 Augustin von Moersperg/Wikimedia Commons; p. 19 De Agostini/A. Dagli Orti/Getty Images; p. 23 Emi Cristea/Shutterstock.com; p. 25 J. Norman Reid/Shutterstock.com; p. 27 Herbert Rose Barraud/Wikimedia Commons; p. 29 (main) villorejo/Shutterstock.com; p. 29 (inset) Sean Gallup/Getty Images News/Getty Images.

Printed in the United States of America

CPSIA compliance information: Batch #CS15GS: For further information contact Gareth Stevens, New York, New York at 1-800-542-2595.

Contents

True Tales? 4

Jacob and Wilhelm Grimm 6

A Famous Book 8

The Tale Begins 10

A Different Tune 12

Disappearance 14

A Story in the Window 16

The Black Death 18

The Children's Crusade 20

A Happier Ending 22

The Moral 24

Pied Poetry 26

Hamelin Today 28

Glossary 30

For More Information 31

Index 32

Words in the glossary appear in **bold** type the first time they are used in the text.

True Tales?

When we hear the words "once upon a time" or "long, long ago," we're swept into a world of magic, wonder, and adventure! Did you ever wonder if stories that start like this could be true?

Legends are stories passed down over many years. They're sometimes presented as factual, but aren't likely to be real. Even if not entirely true, legends can tell us a lot about **culture** and history—and they're fun to hear or read!

Many legends were passed down while people were gathered around fires like this one.

5

Jacob and Wilhelm Grimm

In the early 1800s in Germany, two brothers named Jacob and Wilhelm Grimm decided to **preserve** their country's rich legends and fairy tales. Many were only passed to others by word of mouth, so the Grimms wrote them down. They named their collection of 210 stories *Children's and Household Tales*. It was first published in 1812.

The Grimm brothers couldn't have guessed how important or popular their stories would become. The tales were **translated** into 160 languages and served as **inspiration** for entertainment and art, such as music, comic books, and movies.

The Inside Story

The Japanese created two theme parks featuring the Grimm tales.

The Grimm brothers are sometimes better known as the Brothers Grimm.

7

A Famous Book

In the beginning, the Grimm brothers didn't aim their stories at children. They didn't even want any pictures in their book. When they discovered that children liked their stories, they made them more "kid friendly." Some were still pretty scary, though!

One of these stories is the famous legend of the pied piper. The Grimms called it "The Children of Hameln." Unlike many tales, it's set during a certain year—1284—and in the real town of Hamelin, Germany.

The Inside Story

The Walt Disney Company used Grimm tales for such movies as Cinderella and Snow White.

In German, the town of Hamelin is spelled "Hameln." All kinds of images of the pied piper are found in Hamelin, Germany.

Hamelin

Germany

The Tale Begins

The legend of the pied piper begins in 1284, when a stranger arrived in Hamelin. He wore a coat of many colors, called a pied coat. The stranger said he could rid the town of mice and rats for a certain amount of money. The townspeople agreed.

The stranger took out his **fife** and began to play. Mice and rats came running from every house. He walked to the Weser River, and they followed. The pied piper walked into the river, and still they followed him—until all the mice and rats had drowned!

The Inside Story

Austria and England have similar tales about a rat catcher set in their own countries.

The pied piper played his magical tune, and the mice and rats came running.

A Different Tune

However, the townspeople wouldn't pay the pied piper the amount they had agreed upon. They thought it was too much money. He left angrily, but later returned to Hamelin. This time, he was dressed differently. He began to play a different tune on his fife.

This time, instead of mice and rats, he **lured** the children of Hamelin from their homes! The legend says 130 children followed the piper out of town to a nearby mountain.

The Inside Story

In German, this story is sometimes called "Rattenfänger von Hameln," or "Rat Catcher of Hamelin."

The story says all children over the age of 4 followed the piper.

13

Disappearance

A woman saw the children dancing behind the piper and followed them for a distance out of town. Then, she returned to tell their parents what was happening.

A blind boy and a **deaf** boy soon came back. The blind boy told about the piper's music, but he didn't know where the children had gone. The deaf boy couldn't hear the music, but he showed them where the children had entered a cave in the mountain. However, the children weren't there! They were never seen again.

People wonder if this sad tale is based on a true story.

15

A Story in the Window

Most historians agree that a terrible event happened in Hamelin around 1284. It's said that the townspeople put up a stained-glass window in a church around 1300 showing a group of children and a man wearing many colors. That window no longer exists, but accounts say there was writing on it about "lost children."

A town record from 1384 tells of an event that happened "100 years since our children left." That's 100 years after the date of the pied piper's visit.

The Inside Story

In modern times, the term "pied piper" has come to mean a person who attracts a following of others.

This painting is said to have been copied from the Hamelin stained-glass window. Dating from around 1592, it may be the oldest image of the pied piper.

The Black Death

Some historians believe that the **bubonic plague**, also known as the Black Death, killed the children of Hamelin. Rats that carried **infected** fleas spread this terrible illness, or disease. In stories, the pied piper may have stood for death, taking the children away.

However, rats weren't in the original stories. Historians think they were added in the 1500s. Also, the plague didn't reach Europe until the 1300s, after the events were supposed to have taken place.

It's possible that the Hamelin children caught some other deadly disease besides the Black Death, shown here.

19

The Children's Crusade

The Crusades were a series of wars from the 11th to the 13th century in which Christians fought **Muslims** for control of the city of Jerusalem in the **Middle East**. In 1212, many young people in Europe set out to fight in what was called the Children's Crusade. However, none reached Jerusalem. Some wonder if the children of Hamelin were led away by this Crusade.

However, many now question the events of the Children's Crusade. They even wonder if the people involved were really children!

It's said that many children died of hunger on the Children's Crusade.

A Happier Ending

Yet another **theory** about the Hamelin children is that they just left town! They traveled through or over the mountain and walked to Transylvania, an area in the country of Romania. They settled there and formed their own colony.

Records from that time say that wealthy landowners wanted people to settle on their lands in eastern Europe. They sent people from town to town asking for colonists. Young people from Hamelin may have decided to go.

The Inside Story

Another famous tale is connected to Transylvania–the legend of Dracula!

Transylvania is a beautiful region in the central part of Romania with rich valleys and green mountains.

The Moral

Many fairy tales have a moral, which is a message about how to act in the right way. The moral of the Grimms' pied piper story is that people should keep their word and honor their agreements.

The townspeople promised the piper they would pay him a certain amount for ridding the town of mice and rats. He did what he agreed to do. However, the town wouldn't pay up. If they had paid what they owed, the children would have been safe.

The Inside Story

Today, the saying "pay the piper" means face the **consequences** of your actions.

This pied piper statue is found in Pennsylvania. The story has spread to all parts of the world.

25

Pied Poetry

Robert Browning, a famous poet who lived in the 1800s, wrote a poem called "The Pied Piper of Hamelin." It tells the story of the rats, the pied piper, and the children of Hamelin. Just as in the Grimm story, the townspeople back out of their promise to pay the piper.

Browning ends the poem with the moral: "If we promised them aught [anything], then let us keep our promise." He suggests keeping your promises to everyone—especially to pipers!

The Inside Story

Robert Browning's poem says the children went to Transylvania, though the children can't remember how they got there.

Robert Browning wrote his poem "The Pied Piper of Hamelin" in 1842.

Hamelin Today

Today, Hamelin is a beautiful little German town that looks like the setting of a fairy tale. The streets are painted with rats to point the way to special places. The Pied Piper House stands in the middle of town and is used as a restaurant.

Every Sunday from mid-May to mid-September, a pied piper play is put on at noon outside. Eighty actors retell the story of how a piper led the children away so many years ago.

The Inside Story

There's one street without music in Hamelin. Bungelosenstrasse ("drumless street") doesn't allow it. Supposedly, it was the last street on which the children were seen.

Hamelin has beautiful streets that probably look very much like they did during the lives of the Grimm brothers.

Glossary

bubonic plague: a deadly disease that featured large swellings, called buboes, forming in certain parts of the body

consequence: something that happens as a result of an action

culture: the beliefs and ways of life of a group of people

deaf: not able to hear

fife: a musical instrument that looks like a small flute

infected: having germs inside the body

inspiration: the act of causing someone to want to do something

lure: to draw someone or something closer in order to catch it

Middle East: the area where southwestern Asia meets northeastern Africa

Muslim: a follower of the religion of Islam

preserve: to keep safe or in an original state

theory: an explanation based on facts that is generally accepted

translate: to change the words of one language into another

For More Information

Books

Grimm, Jacob, and Wilhelm Grimm. *The Original Folk and Fairy Tales of the Brothers Grimm: The Complete First Edition.* Trans. Jack Zipes. Princeton, NJ: Princeton University Press, 2015.

Merwin, W. S. *The Book of Fables.* Port Townsend, WA: Copper Canyon Press, 2007.

Morpurgo, Michael. *The Pied Piper of Hamelin.* Somerville, MA: Candlewick Press, 2011.

Websites

Children's Stories
www.howstuffworks.com/Childrens-stories3.htm
Read more children's stories with lessons to learn for everyday life.

Grimm's Fairy Tales
www.cs.cmu.edu/~spok/grimmtmp/
Check out other fairy tales collected by the famous Grimm brothers.

Index

Black Death 18, 19

Browning, Robert 26, 27

bubonic plague 18

children 8, 12, 13, 14, 16, 18, 19,
    20, 21, 22, 24, 26, 28

"Children of Hameln, The" 8

Children's and Household Tales 6

Children's Crusade 20, 21

Crusades 20

fife 10, 12

Grimm Brothers 6, 7, 8, 24, 26, 29

Hamelin, Germany 8, 9, 10, 12, 16,
    17, 18, 19, 20, 22, 26, 28, 29

mice and rats 10, 11, 12, 24

moral 24, 26

mountain 12, 14, 22, 23

Pied Piper House 28

"Pied Piper of Hamelin, The" 26, 27

"Rat Catcher of Hamelin" 12

stained-glass window 16, 17

Transylvania 22, 23, 26